HORSE POWER

SPARKY'S STEM GUIDE TO

DIGGERS

BY KIRSTY HOLMES

KidHaven PUBLISHING

Published in 2023 by **KidHaven Publishing, an Imprint of Greenhaven Publishing, LLC**
29 East 21st Street
New York, NY 10010

Edited by: Emilie Dufresne
Designed by: Danielle Rippengill

Cataloging-in-Publication Data

Names: Holmes, Kirsty.
Title: Sparky's STEM guide to diggers / Kirsty Holmes.
Description: New York : KidHaven Publishing, 2023. | Series: Horse power | Includes glossary and index.
Identifiers: ISBN 9781534540293 (pbk.) | ISBN 9781534540316 (library bound) | ISBN 9781534540309 (6 pack) | ISBN 9781534540323 (ebook)
Subjects: LCSH: Excavating machinery--Juvenile literature.
Classification: LCC TA735.H635 2023 | DDC 621.8'65--dc23

Printed in the United States of America

CPSIA compliance information: Batch #CSKH23: For further information contact Greenhaven Publishing LLC, New York, New York at 1-844-317-7404.

Please visit our website, www.greenhavenpublishing.com. For a free color catalog of all our high-quality books, call toll free 1-844-317-7404 or fax 1-844-317-7405.

IMAGE CREDITS

All images are courtesy of Shutterstock.com, unless otherwise specified. With thanks to Getty Images, Thinkstock Photo and iStockphoto. Cover – NotionPic, A–R–T, logika600, BiterBig, lukpedclub, Rvector, KostyaTimofeev. Sparky – NotionPic, lukpedclub, Rvector. Peggy – NotionPic. Grid – BiterBig. Construction School – Dmi T. 2 – KostyaTimofeev. 5 – Mascha Tace. 6–11 – KostyaTimofeev. 10 & 11 – hvostik. 12 – KostyaTimofeev. 14 & 15 – intararit. 16 – Krishnadas, Cool Vector Maker. 17 – Butterfly Hunter, NEGOVURA, Benjamin Marin Rubio. 18 & 19 – piscari. 20 – Mascha Tace. 22 – Alex_Murphy, Martial Red, bsd, T VECTOR ICONS. 23 – Dmi T.

CONTENTS

WORDS THAT LOOK LIKE <u>this</u> CAN BE FOUND IN THE GLOSSARY ON PAGE 24.

WELCOME TO DRIVING SCHOOL!

My name is Jeremy Sparkplug, but you can call me Sparky. Welcome to the Horses for Courses driving school. Today we will be learning to drive diggers, cranes, and lifters. It's **construction** day!

You'll be learning to drive some of the heaviest and most useful **vehicles** around. If you pass your driving test, you'll earn your Golden Horseshoe. So pay attention: it's time to DRIVE!

LESSON 1:

WHAT IS A DIGGER?

Diggers, cranes, loaders, bulldozers... These mighty machines dig, smash, flatten, and build everything around us, from the tallest towers to the roads under our feet. Each piece of **heavy machinery** has a special job to do.

HORSES FOR COURSES SCHOOL
EARN YOUR HORSESHOES
DRILLING RIG
BULLDOZER
EXCAVATOR
This is Peggy. She's a master builder!

LESSON 2: PARTS OF A DIGGER

This is a digger. Its real name is an excavator. Its main jobs are digging holes and moving heavy things.

CAB

This is where the driver sits. It is on a **rotating** platform.

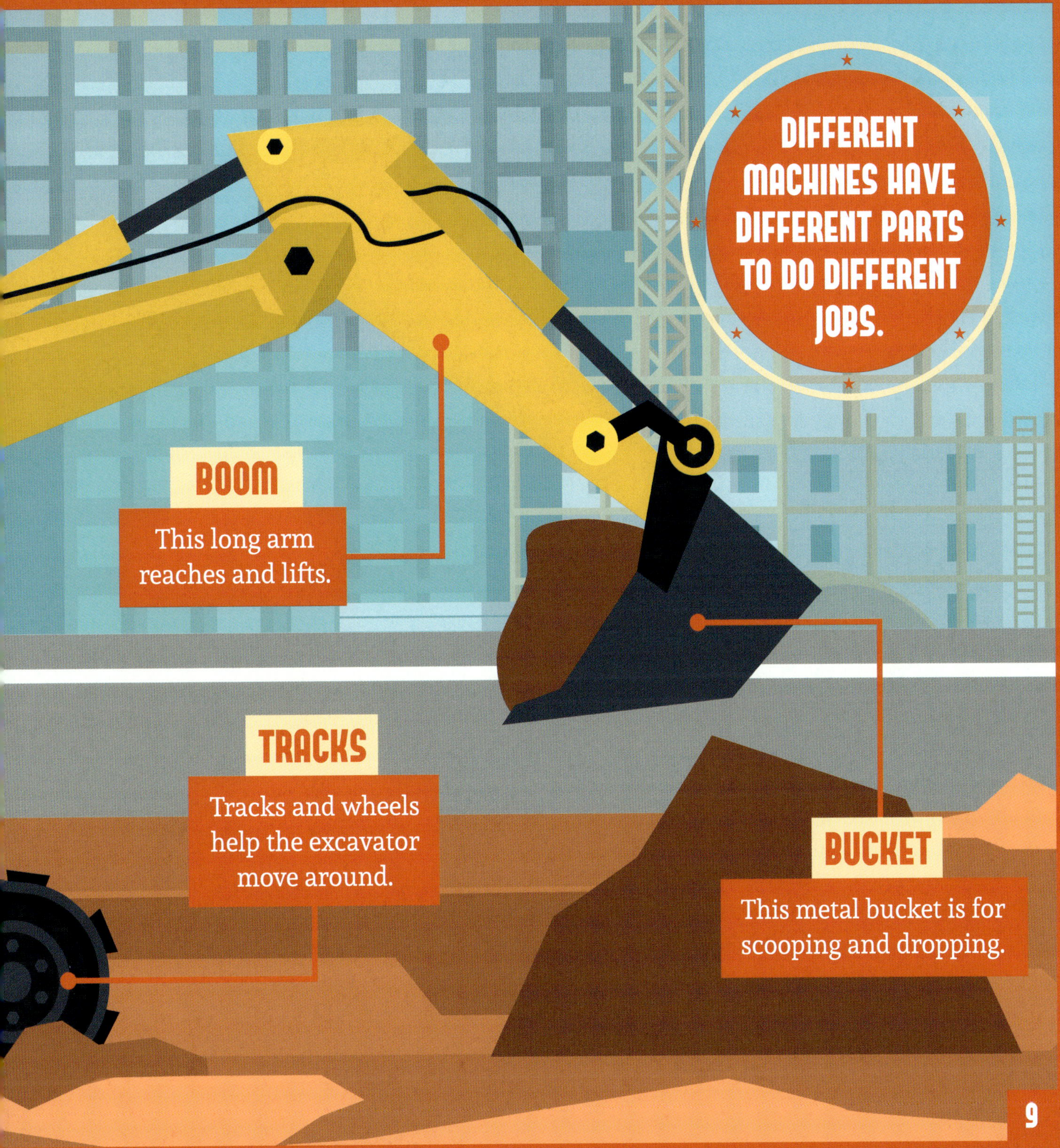
DIFFERENT MACHINES HAVE DIFFERENT PARTS TO DO DIFFERENT JOBS.
BOOM
This long arm reaches and lifts.
TRACKS
Tracks and wheels help the excavator move around.
BUCKET
This metal bucket is for scooping and dropping.

LESSON 3: DRIVING A DIGGER

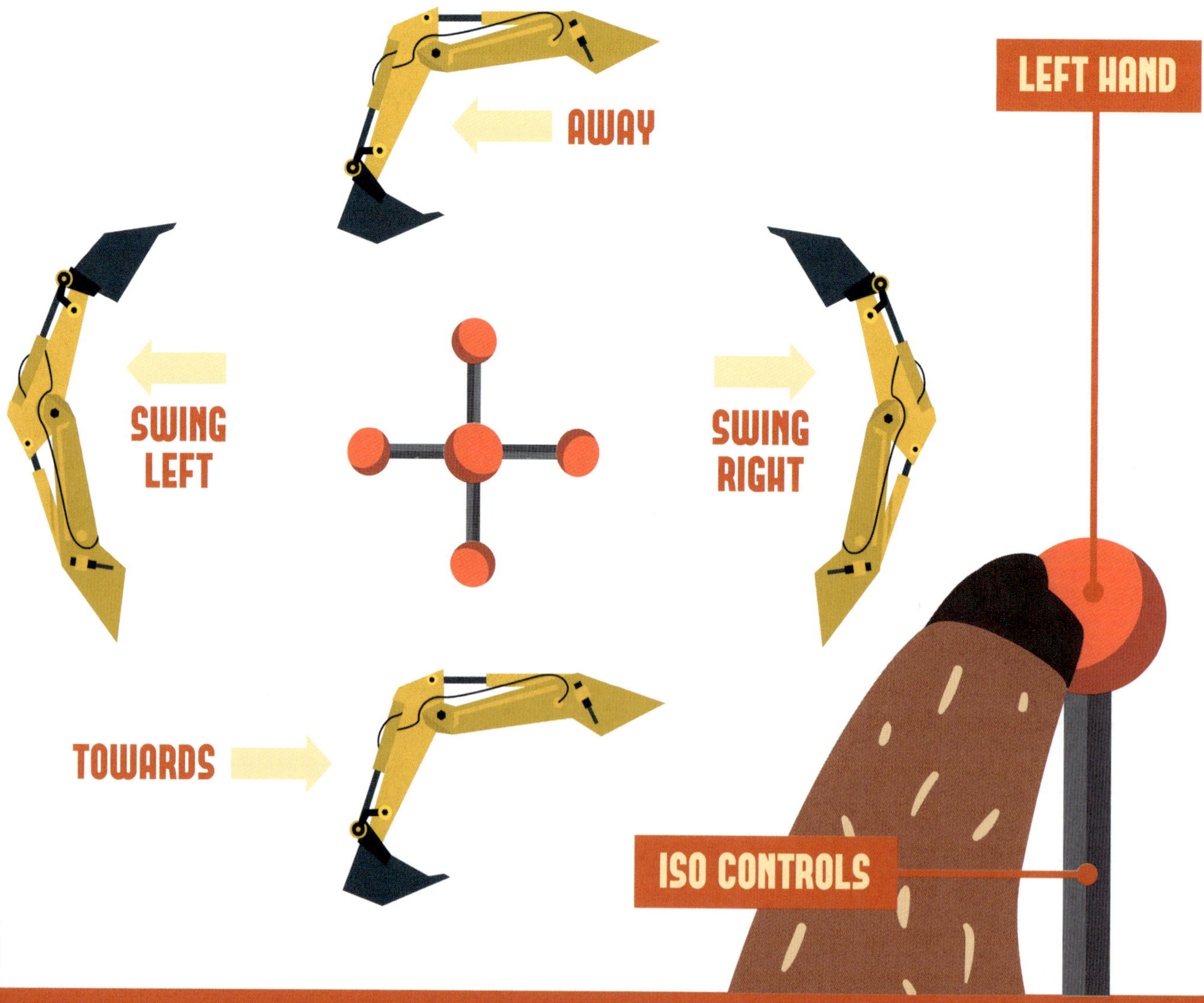

Diggers are controlled using levers and joysticks. The controls on most diggers are the same, so people can drive most diggers without having to learn new controls. In many places around the world, people use the control pattern shown below.

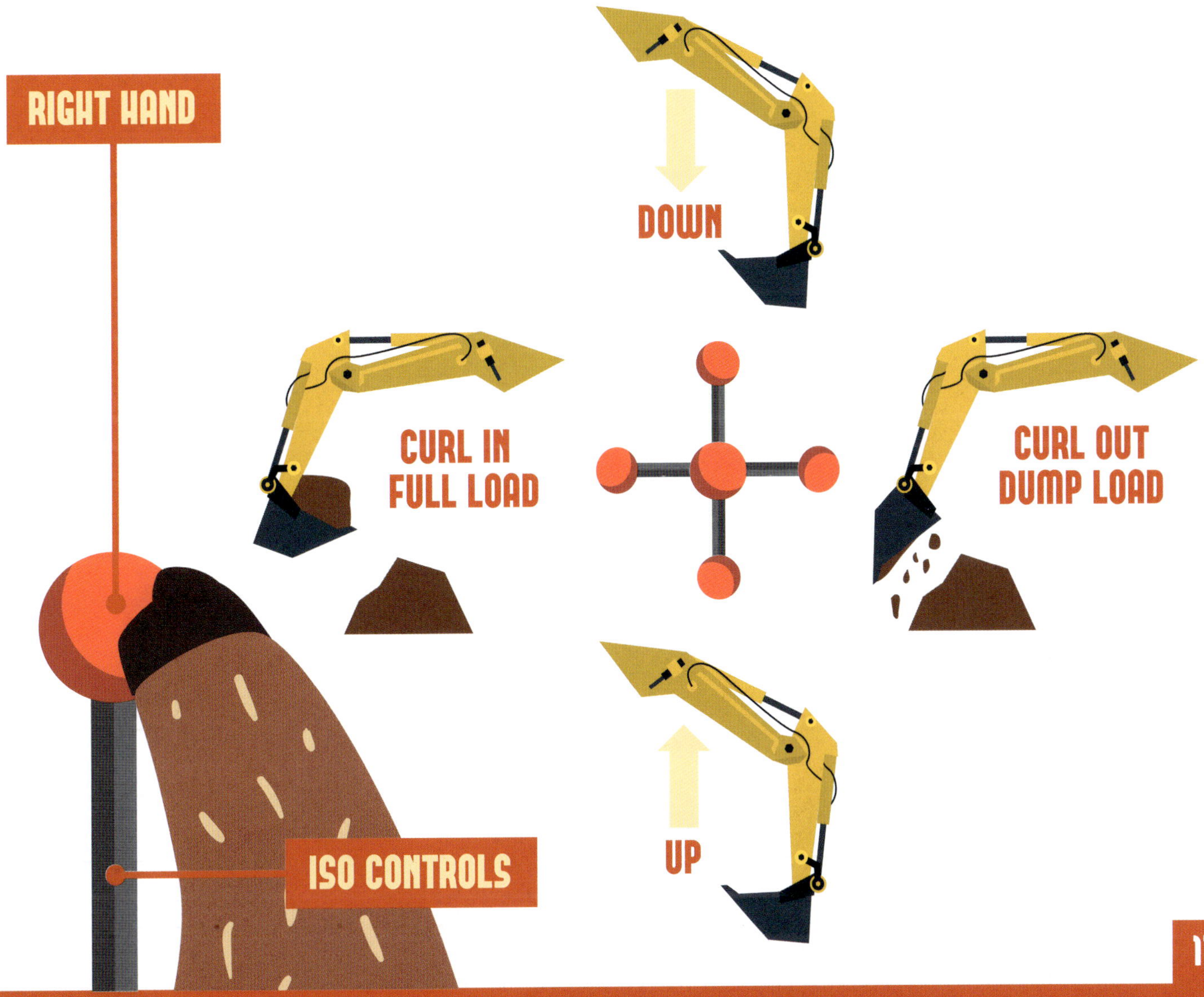

LESSON 4:

DIGGING

Need to dig a big hole, move a big pile of earth, or clear some land so you can build on it? Then you need one of these earthmoving machines.

CHERRY PICKER

These have a platform that can be raised and lowered. Cherry pickers can lift workers or items to high places.

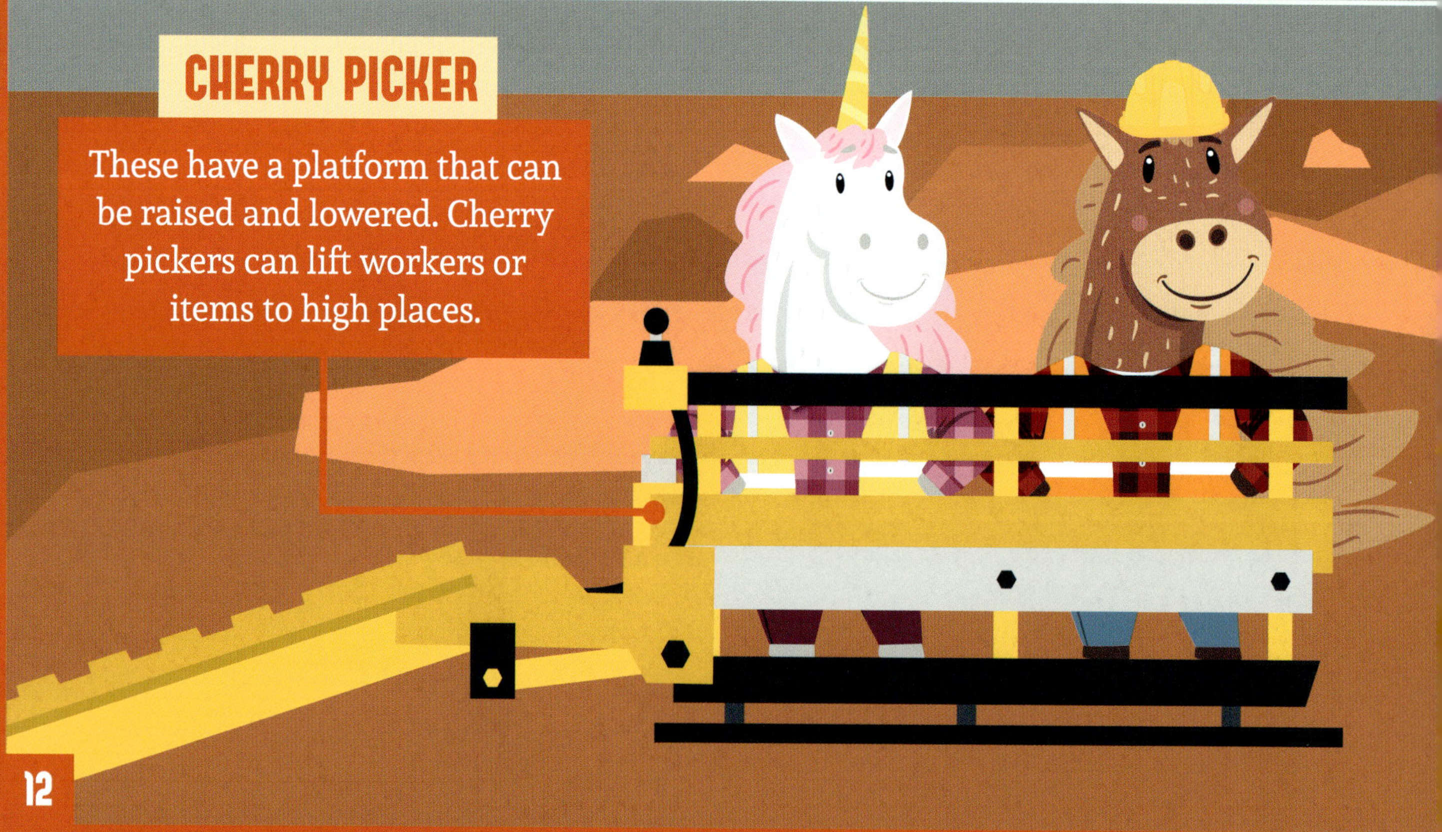

BULLDOZER

A bulldozer is a powerful machine used to push rocks and earth, or knock down buildings and trees. It is like a tractor, but with a big plate on the front.

EXCAVATOR

Excavators can be used to dig, lift, move, crush, clear, and **demolish**.

LESSON 5:

LIFTING

Have you ever looked up at a tall building and wondered how they got the roof on? Lifting machines have the answer...

NO JOB TOO BIG...

Cranes are used to lift large, heavy items to high places. Some of the biggest cranes are found at shipyards, where they load and unload huge **containers** on ships.

...NO JOB TOO SMALL

Other construction vehicles, such as the forklift truck, can be used to lift smaller loads. This one is loading things into a container, ready to be put on the ship by the crane.

LESSON 6:

SITE SAFETY

All these vehicles are really cool. But a construction site is a dangerous place. It is very important that we all look out for these types of signs, which tell us how to stay safe.

YELLOW = DANGER!

Look out for yellow signs, which warn you of dangers.

BLUE = MUST DO

Blue signs tell you things you must do or use to stay safe.

RED = DO NOT!

Red signs mean you must not enter an area, do something, or use something shown on the sign.

GREEN = SAFE

Green signs show you where it is safe to go and what it is safe to do.

Lesson 7:

A Bigger Digger

Some of the biggest vehicles in the world are bucket-wheel excavators. These have a large wheel with buckets on it, which turns and scoops earth, coal, or other things onto a **conveyor belt**.

CAN YOU SPOT PEGGY AND SPARKY BY THE BAGGER 288? LOOK REALLY CLOSELY!

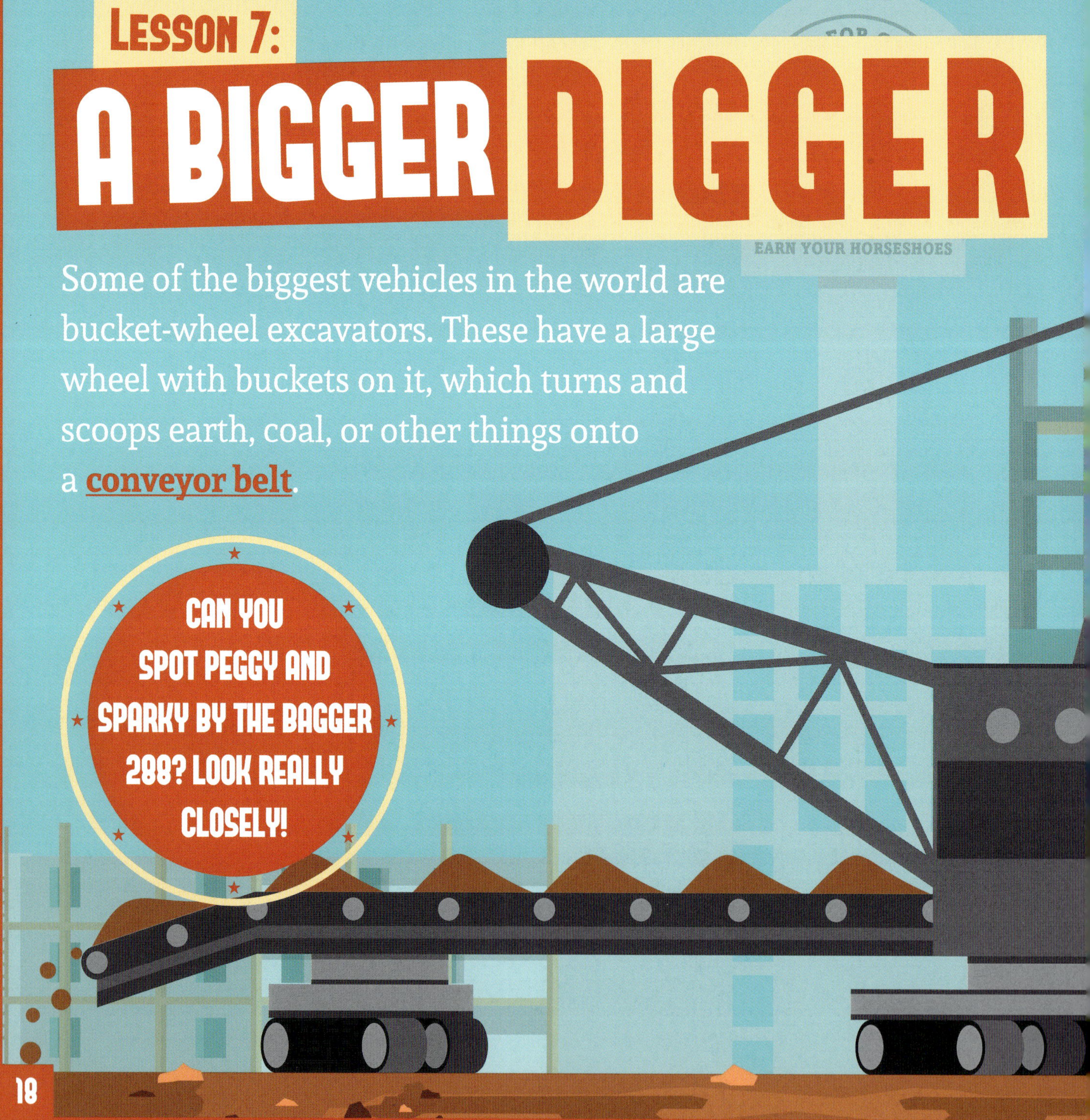

BAGGER 288

The biggest of these giants is the Bagger 288. It is around 315 feet (96 m) tall. It can dig over 264,550 tons (240,000 tonnes) of coal each day. It has a top speed of about 29.5 feet (9 m) per minute – so it won't break any speed records, but it's amazing at doing its job: DIGGING!

DRIVING TEST

Listen up, crew! You've got to pass your driving test if you want to get your hands on these mean machines! (Check your answers on page 21!)

Questions

1. What does the boom on an excavator do?
2. In the control pattern shown on pages 10–11, how do you curl the bucket outward?
3. What does a cherry picker do?
4. What do yellow signs mean?
5. How tall is the Bagger 288?

Did you get them all right?

Of course you did – here is your Golden Horseshoe.
Now do I hear the whistle? Time to get to work!

Answers: 1. Reach and lift 2. Right hand, push right 3. Lifts things high up 4. They warn you of danger 5. About 315 feet tall

Bonus Lesson:

DOUBLE BUNGEE

You mustn't mess around on a building site, and safety is really, really important. However, highly trained, grown-up professionals can use these amazing machines in fun ways...

STEP ONE

Crane

STEP TWO

Rubber bands

STEP THREE

Best friend

STEP FOUR
DOUBLE BUNGEE!
... and don't try this at home!

GLOSSARY

CONSTRUCTION	building works, especially related to a building or structure
CONTAINERS	large boxes that are used to hold things, which are usually transported on boats, trucks, or planes
CONVEYOR BELT	a machine with a moving strap that moves things along
DEMOLISH	to tear down or destroy something, especially a building
HEAVY MACHINERY	heavy-duty vehicles used in construction
ROTATING	spinning or turning around a fixed point
VEHICLES	machines used for carrying or transporting things or people

INDEX